IDEAS IN PSYCHOANALYSIS

Libido

Roger Kennedy

Series editor: Ivan Ward

ICON BOOKS UK

TOTEM BOOKS USA

Published in the UK in 2001
by Icon Books Ltd., Grange Road,
Duxford, Cambridge CB2 4QF
E-mail: info@iconbooks.co.uk
www.iconbooks.co.uk

Published in the USA in 2001
by Totem Books
Inquiries to: Icon Books Ltd.,
Grange Road, Duxford
Cambridge CB2 4QF, UK

Sold in the UK, Europe, South Africa
and Asia by Faber and Faber Ltd.,
3 Queen Square, London WC1N 3AU
or their agents

Distributed to the trade in the USA
by National Book Network Inc.,
4720 Boston Way, Lanham,
Maryland 20706

Distributed in the UK, Europe,
South Africa and Asia by
Macmillan Distribution Ltd.,
Houndmills, Basingstoke RG21 6XS

Distributed in Canada by
Penguin Books Canada,
10 Alcorn Avenue, Suite 300,
Toronto, Ontario M4V 3B2

Published in Australia in 2001
by Allen & Unwin Pty. Ltd.,
PO Box 8500, 83 Alexander Street,
Crows Nest, NSW 2065

ISBN 1 84046 273 6

Series editor: Ivan Ward

Typesetting by Hands Fotoset

Printed and bound in the UK by
Cox & Wyman Ltd., Reading

Introduction: Libido as a Theoretical Concept

Libido is Sigmund Freud's concept of the mental aspect of sexual energy underlying the various transformations of the sexual drives. It is a theoretical concept which, as we shall see, was put forward originally in order to account for pathological clinical observations from neurotic patients, where sexual tensions associated with sexual ideas were seen to have a key role in producing anxiety and other symptoms. Libido came increasingly to have an important place in Freud's theory of the mind and its development. As time went on, he began to include observations from more psychotic illnesses, such as manic depression, hypochondriasis and paranoia. Eventually, libido was to be replaced by Eros, into which it was incorporated, when Freud introduced a theory of sexuality which became both broader in scope and linked to Ancient philosophy. We can see Freud's shifts in theory as a journey from the investigation of the minutiae of his patients' sexual lives to the consideration of the fundamental place of life and death in the human condition.

Libido in Freud's theory of the sexual drives is both a 'quantitative' concept, referring to hypothetical amounts of sexual energy motivating the sexual drives, and a 'qualitative' notion, which means that libido is about specifically sexual drives; it is not to be confused with mental energy in the general sense. In Freud's words, libido is a:

. . . quantitatively variable force which could serve as a measure of processes and transformations occurring in the field of sexual excitation. We distinguish this libido in respect of its special origin from the energy which must be supposed to underlie mental processes in general, and we thus also attribute a qualitative *character to it. . . . [Its] production, increase or diminution and displacement should afford us possibilities for explaining the psychosexual phenomena observed.*[1] (Freud, 1905)

Libido is thus a hypothetical way of measuring the sexual processes, an imagined unit of quantitative measurement; it is a concept. It is what Jacques Lacan,[2] the French psychoanalyst, described as:

A quantity which you don't know how to measure, whose nature you don't know, but which you always assume to be there. This quantitative notion allows you to unify the variation in qualitative effects, and gives some coherence to the manner in which they succeed one another ... [T]*he notion of libido is a form of unification for the domain of psychoanalytical effects* ... [I]*ts use falls within the traditional scope of any and every theory, tending to end up with a world, the* terminus ad quem [end-point] *of classical physics, or a unitary domain, the ideal of Einsteinian physics. We aren't in a position to align our poor little domain with the universal domain of physics, but the libido partakes of the same ideal.*[3] (Lacan, 1978)

Thus we have the notion of libido as a theoretical quantity, which aims to help to explain and give coherence to the field of psychoanalytical effects, in particular those involved with sexuality, or, to be more specific, what Freud called 'Psychosexuality', laying stress on the mental factor in human sexual life (Freud, 1910).[4] It may be difficult to define, and it may be imaginary and unmeasurable, and yet it is a necessary hypothetical concept, just like gravity and mass and space-time are hypothetical concepts, without which physics could not be elaborated.

Freud discusses the nature of libido and other hypothetical concepts in his theoretical framework in his paper on 'Instincts and their Vicissitudes' (1915). He makes the point that, although there is often an assumption that the sciences should be built upon clear and sharply defined basic concepts, in reality the sciences usually start with fairly indefinite concepts in order to grasp observable phenomena. These concepts, such as drives and libido, are more in the nature of conventions, although:

. . . everything depends on their not being arbitrarily chosen but determined by their having significant relations to the empirical material, relations that we seem to sense before we can clearly recognise and demonstrate them. It is only after more thorough investigation of the field of observation that we are able to formulate its basic scientific concepts with increased precision, and progressively so to modify them that they become serviceable and consistent over a wide area.[5] (Freud, 1915)

Thus libido is a theoretical concept, or 'convention', which aims to help make sense of the psychosexual field, however vague and unmeasurable it may be; it represents one aspect of Freud's thought, his wish to make psychoanalysis an organised and even 'scientific' study of psychosexual phenomena. Like the notion of a drive, libido is a scientific concept on the 'frontier' between the mental and the somatic; it is a psychical entity, and yet it refers to bodily phenomena.

Libido in Freud is also concerned with the nature of love and desire, or with lust and sexual appetite, which is what *libido* means in Latin; and here Freud moves away from purely scientific considerations into the precarious field of human emotions. As he wrote:

Libido is an expression taken from the theory of the emotions. We call by that name the energy, regarded as a quantitative magnitude (though not at present actually measurable), of those drives which have to deal with all that may be comprised under the word 'love'.[6] (Freud, 1921)

In ordinary language, we talk of the 'hunger' of the nutritive drive, and so with the sexual drives, we can talk about libido or 'sexual hunger'. People talk about their libido being raised or diminished, when referring to their sexual interest and drive, their wish to have sex, the accumulation of sexual hunger and tension pressing to be satisfied. It may or may not be connected to love for the other person. Indeed, in some people with problems about commitment, their libido may only increase when in a brief relationship; while with others, it is only in the context of a committed relationship that their libido can be raised enough to establish a successful sexual relationship.

On the other hand, as can be seen throughout Ancient Greek literature, the sexual drives can 'drive' people mad, making them blind to their own and other people's interests. Thus the action of Sophocles' play, *Women of Trachis*, reveals the power of sex in determining the fate of the main characters. Deianira, a hitherto faithful and devoted wife, becomes a murderess by mistake, when she attempts to give her unfaithful husband, Heracles, a love-charm to win him back. There is a whole choral ode celebrating the invincible power of love or lust, before which even the Kings of heaven, the underworld and the ocean must bow down.[7] In Sophocles' *Antigone*, one of the main themes is the power of Eros. The chorus sings of Eros that he who has it is mad;[8] it causes several deaths in the play, and makes the king of Thebes, Creon, a broken man, as his son and wife end up killing themselves as a result of its power.

We have seen, then, that Freud's notions about sexuality encompass both an attempt to create a scientific study of psychosexuality, and also more general aspects of the complex emotion of love, which reach back to Ancient literature. Freud's libido, like that of the Greek Eros, can be a blind force driving humans beyond ordinary reason.

No Libido Please, We're British!

In the early years of psychoanalysis, libido was used by Freud in a general sense to cover the hypothetical energy of the sexual drives in much the same way as it is now used in ordinary language, though with various modifications. But with the introduction of the concept of 'narcissism' in 1914, Freud began increasingly to elaborate a complicated theory of libido and its development, which became essential to his whole conceptual framework. By 1920, this libido theory had become assimilated into an even more general theory of the interaction between two basic drives in the life of the mind – Eros, or the life drives, and Thanatos, or the death drives. In due course, I shall discuss aspects of these various psychoanalytic theories, and how they may be related to clinical work. But before that, I will make some general points about the place of libido theory in contemporary psychoanalysis, particularly in Britain, where it seems to have virtually disappeared. I shall ask throughout this book whether or not this act of exclusion misses out vital elements of Freud's thinking, leaving psychoanalysis impoverished as a result, or whether this is just a sign of psychoanalysis having moved on from an outdated theory, more appropriate to the world of nineteenth-century physics.

The issue of the current relevance, or not, of the term 'libido' has to be seen in the context of the current state of psychoanalytic theory, where sexuality as the central issue for psychoanalysis has been replaced by object relations theory, with its emphasis on early development before the child becomes recognisably sexual. Its great advance on classical Freudian theory was to emphasise the importance of the *relationship* between the subject and his environment, particularly the mother–infant relationship, rather than focus only on the inner world of the individual. This theory describes the

. . . subject's mode of relation to the world; this relation is the entire outcome of a particular organisation of the personality, of an apprehension of objects that is to some extent or other fantasied, and of certain special types of defence.[9] (Laplanche and Pontalis, 1967)

Object relations theory is concerned with both the inner world of the subject and the world of others. It concerns itself with the relation of the subject to his or her objects. However, as Gregorio Kohon points out:

It is not only the real relationship with others

that determines the subject's individual life, but the specific way in which the subject apprehends his relationships with his objects (both internal and external). It is always an unconscious relationship to these objects.[10] (Kohon, 1986)

While object relations theory extends the scope of psychoanalysis – by, for example, pointing towards the vast field of infant and child observation and research, which can provide new data and even confirmation of psychoanalytic ideas – the central importance of sexuality in the theory and practice of psychoanalysis seems to have been displaced. In 1995, André Green even wrote a paper asking if sexuality had anything to do with psychoanalysis these days,[11] as it seems to have virtually disappeared in so many ways. He makes the point that direct discussions of sexuality seem to have declined in ordinary clinical presentations, and sexuality itself seems to have become marginalised as a central analytic concept, even though Freud placed it at the centre of psychic development, analytic theory and clinical work. Green argues that the current fashionable focus on object relations, on early development, borderline pathology and techniques drawn from baby observation, obscures the meaning and importance of sexuality in psychoanalytic theory and practice. But he argues that without, for example, the Freudian notion of libido, we cannot account for the variations, extensions, fixations, regressions, time-lags, enmeshings and unravellings of psychic functioning and development.

For Jacques Lacan, libido is an essential element of sexuality and of his own approach to the study of the unconscious. In his view, what Freud intended to make present in the function of this libido was not some generalised primitive mode of thought, 'like some shade of an ancient world surviving in ours'. Rather:

The libido is the effective presence, as such, of desire. It is what now remains to indicate desire – which is not substance, but which is there at the level of the primary process, and

which governs the very mode of our approach.[12]
(Lacan, 1973)

Lacan maintains that the libido is the essential element of the 'primary process', the basic way that the unconscious functions. Freud divided the functioning of the psychical apparatus into the *primary* and *secondary* processes. In the former, psychical energy flows freely from one idea to another, as can be seen in dreams, where one idea may surrender all its energy to another idea by the process of 'displacement', or appropriate the energy of several other ideas by the process of 'condensation'. In the case of the secondary process, psychical energy is more bound, less freely mobile; it coincides with waking thought, judgement and reasoning.[13] Like the primary process, the libido for Lacan is a free current which gets tied down in various ways, organised and tamed by the secondary process.

The playing down of the role of sexuality in favour of early object relations does not only have theoretical consequences but may also deeply influence what psychoanalysts do or do not see in their patients. For example, instead of seeing hysteria as a condition involving a fundamental conflict concerned with sexual impulses, it is often now seen as a condition involving defence mechanisms to keep primitive, psychotic anxieties at bay or under control. As Kohon (1986, 1999) has described,[14] we can understand why psychoanalysts claim not to find hysterics in their consulting rooms. Their patients may be hysterics, but since the theory looks for something else, it can also find something else. Thus the desexualisation of psychoanalytic theory has potentially serious consequences for day-to-day practice.

One could add that current psychoanalytic theory and practice not only often lack the theoretical concept of libido in the technical sense, but also lack it in the ordinary sense of the word; it has become a sexless theory. It is perhaps only French psychoanalysis, with the all-pervasive influence of Jacques Lacan on

French thinking, not to mention the role of French culture, that has preserved the central place of sexuality. For the British in particular, 'No libido, please' could be taken as the slogan for much psychoanalytic work.

This is not to deny the importance of the place of early relationships in the life of the individual, but we could ask if psychoanalysis has gone too far in eliminating drives and sexuality, forgetting that people in the real world fuck, or want to fuck, or can't fuck when they want to!

My own position with regard to the status of a term like libido is that I am not wholeheartedly for its retention, certainly not without modifications and extensions in its place in psychoanalytic theory, which I will propose in due course. There is a problem, however, about trying to find terms which capture the animal nature of our sexual drives and at the same time incorporate the human element, involving sexual feelings and desires, as well as the many transformations and complexities of the sexual drives. Somehow, we need to include aspects of force, need, urgency, the urge to obtain gratification which can come to dominate some people's lives. While libido may be too much linked to a 'fluid' and energetic model, more appropriate for the science of hydraulics, it does nonetheless manage to capture the quality of sexual hunger rather well, and how this hunger has many variations, a multiplicity of aims, with the capacity to be diverted and divided up in various ways. I would also maintain that Freud's theory of libido raises many fundamental issues concerned with the nature of our sexual life – and our mental life in general – that have been too often ignored and that would be worth revisiting. At the very least, we can understand libido historically as an integral element of Freud's theory of the mind.

What follows is a historical exposition of Freud's libido theory, with various interpretations of its meaning and significance based on subsequent analytic thinkers. This will lead to some suggestions for modifying the theory in the light of subsequent developments, without, hopefully, depriving it of its core elements.

Freud's Early Theory of Libido/ The Missing Link

We can follow the first steps towards a theory of libido in the Freud/Fliess correspondence – a fascinating series of letters, including some theoretical sketches, between Freud and his close friend Wilhelm Fliess, which date from 1887 to 1904, spanning the birth and early development of psychoanalysis.

The first recorded mention of libido comes in 'Draft E', a theoretical sketch probably from June 1894, concerning how anxiety originates in 'anxiety neurosis', a type of illness where the patient suffers from chronic and excessive anxiety, with accompanying somatic symptoms such as breathlessness, indigestion, cardiac pains and some phobic features. Freud distinguished anxiety neurosis from hysteria and *neurasthenia*, or what we probably now call 'chronic fatigue syndrome'. The theory is concerned with how psychical sexual tension is transformed into anxiety due to a failure to discharge sexual tension along psychical paths, and how something blocks the psychical elaboration of the sexual excitation.

Freud collects together a number of cases in this draft, with a variety of roots for their anxiety. These include those people suffering from anxiety due to their virginal status, those who are intentionally sexually abstinent who regard everything sexual as abhorrent, those women who are neglected by their husbands or are not satisfied due to lack of potency, women who do not obtain satisfaction due to the practice of coitus interruptus or whose husbands suffer from premature ejaculation, as well as men who practice withdrawal or who turn excessively to masturbation, men whose potency is diminishing but force themselves to have intercourse, and men who have to abstain from sex for neurotic reasons. He asks how all these cases may be brought together, and suggests that:

What recurs in them all is abstinence. Informed by the fact that even [sexually] *anaesthetic women are subject to anxiety after coitus interruptus, one is inclined to say that it is a question of a psychical accumulation of exci-tation – that is,* an accumulation of psychical sexual tension. *The accumulation is the consequence of prevented discharge. Thus anxiety neurosis is a neurosis of damming up . . . And since no anxiety at all is contained in what is accumulated, the fact can also be accounted for by saying that* anxiety *has arisen by* transfor-mation *out of the accumulated sexual tension.*[15] (Freud, 1985)

But, Freud asks, why and how does this trans-formation into anxiety occur? This question preoccupied him throughout his life, and he gave various explanations for it depending on the stage his theorising had reached, although the key issues and much of the explanation remained constant. At this early point in his thinking, he considers it a question of how tension originating inside the body ('endo-genous' tension), such as that arising from hunger, thirst and the sexual drive, is dealt with by means of specific reactions, which prevent the further occurrence of the excitation in the bodily organs concerned. We may picture this tension as growing either continuously or discontinuously, but only being noticed when it has reached a certain threshold. Above this threshold, Freud postulates that it is deployed psychically, that:

. . . *it enters into relation with certain groups of ideas, which then set about producing the specific remedies. Thus psychical sexual tension above a certain value arouses psychic libido, which then leads to coitus, and so forth.*[16]

So far, this fits with the ordinary understanding of libido as an accumulation of tension that presses for release in a specific reaction – for example, intercourse or masturbation. But if the action fails to ensue, the sexual tension and emotion, or *affect*, increases quickly and urgently:

[It] *becomes disturbing, but there is still no ground for its transformation. In anxiety neurosis, however, such a transformation does occur, and this suggests the idea that there things go wrong in the following way. The psychical tension increases, reaches the threshold value at which it can arouse psychic affect; but for several reasons the psychic linkage offered to it remains insufficient: a* sexual affect *cannot be found, because there is something lacking in the psychic determinants. Accordingly, the physical tension, not being psychically bound, is transformed into anxiety. If one accepts the theory so far, one has to insist that in anxiety neurosis there must be a deficit to be noted in sexual affect, in* psychic libido. *And this is confirmed by observation. If this contention is put before women patients, they are always indignant and declare that on the contrary they now have no desire whatever, and similar statements. Men often confirm the observation that since suffering from anxiety they have felt no sexual desire.*[17]

Thus the problem in anxiety neurosis is one of an insufficient or missing psychic linkage, which can be turned into affect by what Freud calls at this point 'psychic working over'. In ordinary life, sexual tension finds an outlet in action such as intercourse. But if there is constantly no outlet for the release of tension, anxiety will occur in those patients who have problems in *working over* sexual tension. Such psychic work can ordinarily deal with the tension appropriately and without causing bodily symptoms. But when such working over cannot occur, then bodily symptoms will arise instead.

Although at this point in his thinking, Freud's concepts are still developing, much of his approach to how sexual psychic tension becomes transformed into anxiety, due to a lack of the ordinary linking processes in the mind, will be retained in various ways. The basic technique of psychoanalysis, involving trying to find words for disturbing feelings, can be seen as offering links where they are missing. From this point on, the theory behind the practice will become increasingly elaborate and reworked, but the clinical basis for it will remain.

Elaboration of Libido Theory/ Dammed Libido

Freud's book 'Three Essays on the Theory of Sexuality' (1905) stands with the *Interpretation of Dreams* (1900) as his most original contribution to human knowledge. Yet the essays are somewhat difficult to digest because, in the form in which they are now read, there are many additions and revisions, a whole series of different layers added to the original text. Nonetheless, the basic tenets of psychoanalytic theory are there to be seen, and, in particular, the cardinal role of the investigation of sexuality in the life of the human subject, and libido theory, have a key place in this investigation. Years later, in his fourth edition of the book, written in 1920, Freud states that despite the changes to psychoanalytic thinking, the basic findings from the three essays remain intact, despite attempts by some to

. . . abandon it and to adopt fresh views which were intended to restrict once more the part played by the factor of sexuality in normal and pathological sexual life.[18]

His first essay is concerned with observations from the sexual 'aberrations', mainly perversions of various kinds, as well as observations from homosexual and neurotic patients. The second essay deals with infantile sexuality, and the third essay covers the transformations of puberty. Because of the complexity of the text, I can pick out only a few relevant themes.

Overall, what comes through from the book is an attempt to capture the great variety of sexual life, the place of biological elements in the subject's sexual life, the many aims of the sexual drives, the plasticity, fluidity and complexity of sexual feelings, and the precarious way in which the sexual organisation is united at puberty out of various fragmentary elements. Normal sexual life is shown to consist of many potentially perverse elements, perversion occurring when one of these elements begins to dominate over the others.

Libido, which was introduced as a term to indicate a kind of sexual hunger, is shown to flow in many different ways, to change from one object to another with apparent ease, like, we could add, the primary process. It is shown to have its sources in many different parts of the body, and to be a major source of anxiety and symptoms in neurotic patients. Libido is shown to pass through a long course of development, with many breaks, and hence many possibilities for that development to be interfered with.

But, when libido fails to find satisfaction, it can behave

. . . like a stream whose main bed had become blocked. It proceeds to fill up collateral channels which hitherto had been empty.[19]

These 'collateral channels' become the source of various perverse tendencies in neurotic patients. It is notable that Internet porn sites are categorised more or less according to these collateral channels. Sexual practices which in limited amounts are a normal part of sexual life – such as the use of the mouth, the anus, touching and looking, and some elements of sadism and masochism – may come to dominate sexual life to the exclusion of everything else, as if the collateral channel takes over from the main stream and dominates the subject in a tyrannical way, overwhelming his or her sexual life so that ordinary intercourse may not be possible. It is as if one 'site' (on the Internet or the body) comes to dominate the subject's sexual life. The subject's libido is said to be 'fixated' at a particular stage of development – the moment, as it were, when the diversion from the main stream of libido took place.

Elsewhere, Freud gives a vivid example of such a fixation as the cause of foot fetishism. The patient was a man who . . .

. . . is to-day quite indifferent to the genitals and other attractions of women, but who can be plunged into irresistible sexual excitement only by a foot of a particular form wearing a shoe. He can recall an event from his sixth year which was decisive for the fixation of his libido. He was sitting on a stool beside the governess who was to give him lessons in English. The governess, who was an elderly, dried-up, plain-looking spinster, with pale-blue eyes and a snub nose, had something wrong with her foot that day, and on that account kept it, wearing a velvet slipper, stretched out on a cushion. Her leg itself was most decently concealed. A thin, scraggy foot, like the one he had then seen belonging to this governess, thereupon became (after a timid attempt at normal sexual activity at puberty) his only sexual object; and the man was irresistibly attracted if a foot of this kind was associated with other features besides which recalled the type of the English governess.[20]

The fixation of his libido was the cause of his

foot fetishism. One could add here that the fixation of this patient was in the context of a particular form of object relationship, the 'type' of the English governess, someone who obviously took the place of a parent. There may well have been traumatic issues related to his parenting that were projected onto the governess at that particular moment, making his libido particularly susceptible to fixation.

Such fixations due to childhood scenes of various kinds are not uncommon in these and other perversions, though one should add that it is not generally so easy to locate one scene as the main factor behind the perversion. There is usually a whole set of complex factors – in both the family and the individual – at work in perversion and neurosis, many of them obscure, and often involving one or more traumatic episodes. There is a complex interaction between the subject's personality or constitution and the external environment, an interaction which forms their history.

In Freud's 1912 paper on types of onset of

neurosis, he attempts to clarify some of these obscurities by outlining the changes relating to the subject's libido which bring about the outbreak of neurotic illness. His aim in the paper is to

. . . *show that neurotic disposition lies in the history of the development of the libido, and to trace back the operative factors in that development to innate varieties of sexual constitution and to influences of the external world experienced in early childhood.*[21]

Various factors are cited as the precipitating causes of the onset of a neurosis. The first is 'frustration', from an external obstacle and/ or an internal obstacle. With the external obstacle, the subject is healthy so long as their need for love is satisfied by a real object in the external world. But when the object is lost or withdrawn, illness may take place if there is no substitute. With this type, to which, Freud adds, the majority of people belong, the possibility of falling ill only arises when there is abstinence. Frustration has a pathogenic effect because it 'dams up' libido, increasing sexual tension. The subject can remain healthy if he can transform this tension into active energy and find a way of satisfying his libido again, for example by finding a replacement for the lost love-object. Or else, like Alberich in Wagner's *Ring Cycle*, who renounced love in order to steal the Rhinemaidens' gold, he can renounce libidinal satisfaction, 'sublimating the dammed-up libido and turning it to the attainment of aims which are no longer erotic and which escape frustration'.[22]

Frustration, if persistent, can bring into play factors in the personality which hitherto had lain dormant. The person may begin to turn away from reality and become absorbed by the world of phantasy, creating new wishful structures which revive the traces of earlier, particularly infantile elements. Excessive phantasying may cause the libido to move on a backward path, causing 'regression' along infantile lines. A conflict between the subject's present-day way of functioning and these infantile elements may precipitate a neurotic illness.

Frustration due to internal factors arises from elements of previous development: in particular, previous fixations of the libido, which cause at some point in his life a difficulty for the subject in adapting to the demands of reality. Freud gives examples to illustrate the types of situation to which he is referring. These include:

A young man who has hitherto satisfied his libido by means of phantasies ending in masturbation, and who now seeks to replace a régime approximating to auto-erotism by the choice of a real object – or a girl who has given her whole affection to her father or brother and who must now, for the sake of a man who is courting her, allow her hitherto unconscious incestuous libidinal wishes to become conscious – or a married woman who would like to renounce her polygamous inclinations and phantasies of prostitution so as to become a faithful consort to her husband and a perfect mother to her child.[23]

All of these people can fall ill if the earlier fixations of their libido are powerful enough to dominate their lives, particularly if, as with the first kind of frustration, they meet with an external obstacle such as a loss of various kinds. Furthermore, some people remain permanently 'inhibited' in their development; their libido has never left these earlier infantile fixations.

Freud adds a final example of people who appear to fall ill spontaneously, having been hitherto healthy. A closer consideration of these cases does, however, reveal that a change has indeed taken place in them, and this change is related to them having reached a particular period of life, such as puberty or the menopause, where biological processes come into play. Then, the

. . . quantity *of libido in their mental economy has experienced an increase which is in itself enough to upset the equilibrium of their health and to set up the necessary conditions for a neurosis.*[24]

Such a situation is fairly typical of those adolescents who break down at or near to puberty, or first show signs of disturbance at this time. Their earlier life may appear to have been relatively normal, or at least there has been no overt disturbance; but it is the powerful emergence of sexual feelings, and the attempts to deal with them, that become the driving force for adolescent turmoil. Eros can drive the adolescent mad, to recall the theme from Greek literature.

To give a brief example from an analysis of an adolescent boy. 'Simon' came into analysis at the age of 17 following a suicide attempt. While feeling hopeless and depressed, he had gone to a park and cut his wrists with a razor blade, with the intention of severing an artery. He reported later that the pain of the cut stopped him. He had made a previous attempt to cut an artery a year previously. The first overt sign of disturbance had been at puberty at the age of 13, when he had probably attempted suicide by suffocation with a plastic bag.

The analysis subsequently pieced together that prior to the cutting he had been feeling depressed, and sexually and physically inadequate following a rejection by a girl he liked. He was also, from puberty onwards, greatly troubled by sexual feelings and fantasies. Related to his sexual anxieties, Simon described intense self-hatred, particularly a hatred of and wish to disown his body, which he felt was not masculine enough. He wished at times that he could have another body. His childhood was not marked by any particular disturbance, though his mother always tended to infantilise him, calling him her 'cute little boy'; while his father remained a rather distant and cut-off figure, depressed and unavailable.

One of the main themes of his analysis was how he became threatened by the emergence of sexual feelings at puberty, which precipitated the first outbreak of symptoms. He subsequently began to attack his maturing body through cutting, in part as a way of trying to cling onto the old immature body image. Important therapeutic work was done by focusing on the dynamic interplay between Simon's wish to avoid growing up and his need to accept the reality of his maturing body, as well as beginning to deal better with his sexual desires, or the quantity of libido driving him.

The damming-up of libido is for Freud a basic factor in the production of a neurosis, which can open up paths to regression, causing conflict and neurosis. In Simon's case, the damming up could be seen to open up his regressive wishes to remain a child and to attack his maturing body. Freud adds that we are reminded here that the quantitative factor should not be left out in any consideration of the precipitating causes of illness, and that all the other factors – frustration, fixation and developmental inhibition – remain ineffectual unless:

. . . they affect a certain amount of libido and

bring about a damming-up of libido of a certain height. It is true that we are unable to measure this amount of libido which seems to us indispensable for a pathogenic effect; we can only postulate it after the resulting illness has started.[25]

Once more, we can see how crucial to Freud is his emphasis on the role of the quantity of libido in creating conditions for the outbreak of a neurosis; the damming-up of libido leads to collateral channels being opened up in the mind, particularly channels which had been basically closed up in childhood.

While this is a vivid description of what may take place when a neurosis breaks out, one may ask whether it is to be taken literally, or how much it can be seen as metaphor. Clearly, Freud is very much of his time, when the general principles of physics were considered to be at the basis of psychology; in order to claim respectability and credibility for a theory of mental functioning, one had to make some link with basic scientific concepts, such as that of quantities of energy. Indeed, to a great extent, this demand for scientific credibility remains with us today. However, one can also ask whether the use of the concept of hypothetical amounts of libido as anything other than a metaphor may be stretching the claims for scientific credibility too far, particularly as Freud admits that it is unmeasurable. Why use libido at all when it is only a hypothetical quantitative concept? Would we lose anything by dropping its use?

Because of the uncertainties about the status of libido, we can easily appreciate why it has now fallen into disuse, at a time when psychoanalysis is often under attack for being either unscientific or, worse, pseudo-scientific. However, a main point to make is that libido has a crucial role in Freud's theory, at least in the early and middle phases of his thought. It has a place as a key term, or signifier, in the network of other signifiers. Removing it means shifting the meaning of all the other terms he uses; it would also, as we shall see, make unintelligible the understanding of the place of narcissism in the development of his theory. But, we can still ask, is that a good enough reason to retain the term? Is its use only of historical interest? Or perhaps it is best seen as a useful, even metaphorical, way of capturing the experience of sexual life in terms which make sense, and which also link up with its use in the ordinary language of everyday life.

Development of the Libido/Stages in Life's Way

We have alluded to the fact that the libido develops, and that there may be regressions backwards to earlier developmental stages in the outbreak of neurotic illness. In the early editions of the 'Three Essays', Freud emphasises his discovery of infantile sexuality. This concept arose because memories and associations arising from the analysis of adults regularly led back to the early years of childhood. Later, for example in his case study on Little Hans in 1909, and then from direct observations by child analysts, there was some confirmation of his theory. Infantile sexuality is to be seen long before the genital organs come to dominate sexual life; that is, it is an important element of the 'pregenital organisation' of the libido. Such sexuality involves parts of the body, or what Freud called 'erotogenic zones', which can become the seat of pleasurable excitations. Such zones can be any part of the skin or mucous membrane capable of being the source of pleasure. The child passes through overlapping stages, where one after the other an erotogenic zone first dominates and then is overtaken by another leading zone.

At the oral stage, thumb-sucking is one of the earliest sexual manifestations of childhood, in which the child is searching for pleasure and comfort. It is a kind of substitute for the earlier intense pleasure of sucking at the mother's breast. Freud thus describes an oral sexuality at this stage of development. He also then describes the activity of the anal zone as providing pleasure. Thus:

*Children who are making use of the suscept-
ibility to erotogenic stimulation of the anal zone
betray themselves by holding back their stool till
its accumulation brings about violent muscular
contractions and, as it passes through the anus,
is able to produce powerful stimulation of the
mucous membrane. In so doing, it must no
doubt cause not only painful but also highly
pleasurable sensations.*[26] (Freud, 1905)

However, it was only gradually in Freud's
theory that the libido's development was to be
described as a series of successive, if overlapping, stages: the famous oral, anal, phallic
and genital stages. In the original 1905 edition
of 'Three Essays', Freud merely described an
'auto-erotic' stage before object-choice has taken
place, and when the infant obtains pleasure
solely from parts of its own body, through for
example sucking or masturbation.

It is worth making the point here that in Freud
the issue of development is complex – something which is often ignored. It is not merely a

question of a sequence of stages. Development in Freud is not a simple linear model, with one stage clearly following another, but a complex model, with constant interaction between the past and the present, and with the mind constantly reordering past experiences in the light of present circumstances. There are present in this model what one could call two kinds of history – the history of events and the history of layers. The history of events is the traditional kind of history as a linear narrative, with one event following another in linear time. The history of layers involves looking at history as a succession of shifting layers, as fragments of living reality, where, as in the unconscious, distinctions between the past and the present may be merged. During an analysis, associations from many different layers of the mind may emerge. Putting the associations into some kind of understandable linear narrative – the history of events – is also an important part of the clinical work, and involves the secondary process. But it is the history of layers which is the main generator of new connections and meanings, with some layers of the mind following directly from one another in time, while others merge, and yet others stand out in apparent isolation. The human subject can retrieve elements from many different layers.

An example of this can be seen in a session from a patient of mine near to the ending of her analysis. She had come because of anxiety symptoms, and had difficulties with being emotionally in touch with herself and her children. A mid-week session began with two dreams. In the first dream, Monday and Friday were rolled into one, with no gap between them. There was food around but she felt it was not good enough. Her immediate associations were that this was indicative of her attitude of avoiding what was on offer, and forgetting what was on offer when there were breaks in the analysis. In the second dream, I appeared and said that she should be grateful that I was so tolerant of her. Then I gave her something, a key or a bill. She then held onto my finger. Her associations were to her feelings about the difficulty she had in dealing with break-ups, and her fear that, with the impending ending of the analysis, *everything* would come to an end.

In the session, we explored her early oral level of development, corresponding to her needy, dependent side, an area with which she had had considerable difficulty. She replied that she often felt that things were slipping away from her; her mind felt like a sieve, so that everything of value passed through it; but she now suddenly saw the damage that came from pulling herself and others to pieces. She recalled some memories from childhood where she had constantly been self-destructive in this way. This led to some acknowledgement about the anger she felt about being left by me. She was then able to admit that there were positive things she got from the analysis, that is that there were other levels involved in what we were doing, not just the early needy oral level. For example, she free-associated that my index finger in the dream felt like something she was trying to hold on to; she was holding my finger for fear of being dropped, but also as something helpful. At this level, she was thus able to see me as separate from her, rather than muddled up with her fantasy of me as before. She added that it was also like the Michelangelo picture of the creation of Adam, with God touching Adam's finger, so that there was the possibility of something creative happening between us.

Overall, one could say with her that there were themes from a number of different layers of her mind; the problem for her was that she tended to want them to be perfectly ordered and indexed, rather than allow them to emerge spontaneously. The work of the analysis, right to the end, was very much about trying to challenge the rigidity of her selective processes.

Marcel Proust gives a description of the human personality which captures rather well what we mean about retrieving layers of the past:

A thing which we saw, a book which we read at a certain period does not merely remain for ever conjoined to what existed then around us; it remains also faithfully united to what we ourselves then were and thereafter it can be handled only by the sensibility, the personality that were then ours . . . So that my personality of today may be compared to an abandoned quarry, which supposes everything it contains to be uniform and monotonous, but from which memory, selecting here and there, can, like some Greek sculptor, extract innumerable statues.[27]

The basis for Freud's complex view of human development can be seen already in the Freud/ Fliess correspondence, where, in 1896, Freud described how memory traces are constantly being rearranged in accordance with fresh circumstances, a process which he called 'retranscription'.[28]

A year later, he describes the role of 'deferred action', *Nachträglichkeit*, in which early memories and experiences are revised and rearranged at a later date in order to fit in with fresh experiences, or with new developmental stages.

In his 1899 paper on 'Screen Memories', Freud questions whether we

. . . *have any memories at all* from *our childhood: memories* relating *to our childhood may be all that we possess. Our childhood memories show us our earliest years not as they were but as they appeared at the later periods when the memories were aroused. In these periods of arousal, the childhood memories did not . . .* emerge; *they were* formed *at that time.*[29]

It was only some years later in the 'Wolf Man' case that Freud returned to this notion, where he emphasised how a scene from early life can become traumatic later, and how *Nachträglichkeit* has the effect of making the patient disregard time. Thus Freud writes of the Wolf Man:

At the age of one and a half the child receives an impression to which he is unable to react adequately; he is only able to understand it and

to be moved by it when the impression is revived in him at the age of four; and only twenty years later, during the analysis, is he able to grasp with his conscious mental processes what was then going on in him. The patient justifiably disregards the three periods of time, and puts his present ego into the situation which is so long past.[30] (Freud, 1918)

Thus the psychoanalytic concept of development does not merely refer to processes involving linear time, but, in addition, to a different kind of time – psychical time – where past and present are constantly being re-organised by the human subject. Furthermore, we can say that sexual life is bound up with a special kind of temporality, because the sexual drives go through what Freud called a 'diphasic' development.[31] That is, the onset of sexual development in humans occurs in two phases – the childhood period, followed by the so-called 'period of latency', in which sexual urges die down, before re-emerging at puberty. Childhood sexual issues can thus be reorganised in the light of the subsequent period of puberty, involving a reworking of what has gone before. Such re-working at adolescence may enable earlier conflicts to be potentially resolved, making adolescence a period where the subject may have a 'second chance' to deal with the past.

Lacan emphasised that the stages of libido development are tied to the subject's history. The so-called stages are to be seen within the context of the developing child's attempt to place themselves within a family and societal structure, and are also to be seen in the context of the adult's subsequent reorganisation of memory. The stages can be seen as nodes or turning points in the subject's attempts to recognise their history.

Thus, every fixation at a so-called instinctual stage is above all a historical scar: a page of shame that is forgotten or undone, or a page of glory that compels.[32] (Lacan, 1966)

Furthermore, Lacan writes that these stages are

already organised in subjectivity, that is within a symbolic structure involving relations between subjects; even before it is born, the child has a place in the parents' minds, possibly even a name. There is a family history, an organisation into which he will have to fit, or not.

And, to put it clearly, the subjectivity of the child who registers as victories and defeats the heroic chronicle of the training of his sphincters, enjoying the imaginary sexualization of his cloacal orifices, turning his excremental expulsions into aggressions, his retentions into seductions, and his movements of release into symbols – this subjectivity is not fundamentally different *from the subjectivity of the psychoanalyst who, in order to understand them, tries to reconstitute the forms of love he calls pregenital . . . In other words, the anal stage is no less purely historical when it is actually experienced than when it is reconstituted in thought, nor is it less purely grounded in intersubjectivity. On the other hand, seeing it as a mere stage in some instinctual maturation leads even the best minds off the track.*[33]

Melanie Klein added to the complexity of how these stages can be viewed when she reworked the concept of 'developmental stage' into the concept of 'position'.[34] A position, such as the paranoid-schizoid or the depressive position, is an organisation of defences, phantasies, object relationships, anxieties; it is a mental space in which the subject can be located at any time in their life. The subject can go in and out of positions throughout their life. There remains, for example, the potential to re-experience psychotic anxieties from early development; these anxieties are not simply overcome in the course of development, but remain potentially available, and liable to be re-experienced whenever the subject comes against certain critical situations, such as loss, frustration and the demands of being in psychoanalytical treatment.

To return specifically to the nature of libido development, it was in his 1913 paper, 'The

Disposition to Obsessional Neurosis', that Freud delineated a separate anal-sadistic stage of the pregenital organisation, as a result of observations from obsessional neurotic patients. He highlights in these patients the extraordinary part played by impulses of hatred and anal erotism. He gives a fairly sketchy and rather unusual clinical example to illustrate his theme. This was of a woman patient who began, after some traumatic experience, to develop an anxiety hysteria, but who, one day, suddenly developed an obsessional neurosis which displaced the hysteria. The new neurosis was a reaction to a new problem relating to her current sexual life.

Freud describes how the patient

. . . *had been a happy and almost completely contented wife. She wanted to have children, from motives based on an infantile fixation of her wishes, and she fell ill* [with anxiety attacks] *when she learned that it was impossible for her to have any by her husband who was the only object of her love . . . Her husband understood, without any admission or explanation on her part, what his wife's anxiety meant; he felt hurt, without showing it, and in his turn reacted neurotically by – for the first time – failing in sexual intercourse with her. Immediately afterwards he started on a journey. His wife believed that he had become permanently impotent, and produced her first obsessional symptoms on the day before his expected return.*[35]

Her obsessional symptoms involved scrupulous washing and cleanliness, and protective measures against severe injuries which she thought others should fear from her – which Freud suggested were reaction formations against her own anal-erotic and sadistic impulses. That is, the wanting to be clean was a reaction to the anal impulses, and the fear of retaliation a reaction to her own sadistic impulses.

As Freud describes:

Her sexual need was obliged to find expression in these shapes after her genital life had lost all its value owing to the impotence of the only man of whom there could be any question for her.[36]

He then adds to the clinical picture the fact that the patient's sexual life began in early childhood with beating phantasies. Then:

After they were suppressed, an unusually long period of latency set in, during which the girl passed through a period of exalted moral growth, without any awakening of female sexual feelings. Her marriage, which took place at an early age, opened a time of normal sexual activity. This period, during which she was a happy wife, continued for a number of years, until her first great frustration [of not having children] brought on the hysterical neurosis. When this was followed by her genital life losing all its value, her sexual life . . . returned to the infantile stage of sadism.[37]

Once more, we can see how Freud's theory is intimately related to concrete issues of people's daily sexual lives, something which is too often ignored these days.

Abraham, one of Klein's analysts, wrote two key papers on the development of the libido. The first, in 1916, gives evidence for the oral stage from the analysis of psychotic patients, while the second, in 1924, to which we shall return later, is a comprehensive account of the stages of libido development in relation to the various stages of object-love. The latter paper particularly influenced Klein and laid the basis for her own theory of object relations.

In his earlier paper on 'The First Pregenital Stage', Abraham makes observations on the oral stage of development, based on the psycho-analysis of ill patients, in whom such early experiences seem particularly available. It is worthwhile giving some details from this paper as it also reveals particularly clearly the clinical basis both for libido theory and for psycho-analytical theory in general.

Abraham first gives clinical material from the analysis of a schizophrenic patient with a family history of schizophrenia. This patient is described as preoccupied with himself in a markedly narcissistic manner in that the slightest fancy, a pun on a word, etc., could occupy him intensely and for long periods of time, while his own physical condition absorbed his interest more than anything else. His genital and anal sensations were of the highest importance to him. Moreover, he was addicted to anal as well as genital masturbation. During the period of puberty he derived pleasure from playing with faeces, and later on he occupied himself with his bodily excretions. For instance, he took pleasure in eating his own semen.

But it was his oral preoccupations that were of primary interest to the patient. He would wake up from exciting dreams with what the patient called 'oral pollutions', with saliva dribbling from his mouth. He was preoccupied with the love of milk, sucking fluid and his own tongue. He often used to wake at night with intense sexual desires, which could often be assuaged by drinking milk. He felt that his longing to suck milk was his deepest and most primitive need, to which genital masturbation, however pleasurable, was secondary (Abraham, 1916).[38]

Abraham further describes the presence in the patient of what he himself called 'cannibalistic ideas', which went back to early childhood when he had associated loving somebody with eating something good. It seemed to him that he wanted a substitute for human flesh – unlike Hannibal Lecter who actually wanted the real thing – and his associations led to the phantasy of biting into the breast. Abraham adds that the period during which he was nursed at the breast had been unusually full of important occurrences, with constant changes of wet-nurses, and the prolonging of the period of breast-feeding:

These events were bound to have an effect on a child in whose sexual constitution the mouth zone was so strongly accentuated. They must have facilitated the fixation of the libido on an earlier stage or its regression to such a stage.[39]

Thus the characteristics of this case – the predominant importance of the oral zone, the intimate connection between the sexual and nutritive functions, and the strong presence of desires to incorporate the love-object – can be seen to be the same characteristics which Freud attributed to the earliest stages of libidinal development in infancy. While clearly this patient is highly abnormal, the extreme nature of his symptoms renders intelligible phenomena which we can see in other people in a less marked or a more disguised form – for example, in the patient I described who was coming to the end of her analysis, and who brought up issues around orality, as well as other areas. Abraham also discusses the presence of oral fixations in more neurotic patients, such as those pre-occupied with eating and food, persistent thumb-suckers, and patients in whom the sucking habit may become abnormally domi-nant. One could obviously add smokers to his list, including of course Freud himself, who was a persistent cigar smoker.

In summary, Abraham gives a vivid clinical paper illustrating, through the use of remarkable clinical examples, the existence of the oral stage in the development of the libido, and, in particular, the existence of an early cannibalistic stage in this development.

Freud's 1911 paper on paranoia – his commentary on the Schreber case – and Judge Schreber's own memoirs of his psychotic illness also provide examples of how libido theory can help to explain adult symptoms. For example, Schreber describes how he is attached to God by means of divine rays. Freud makes the point that these rays can be seen as the concrete representation and projection outwards of libidinal connections. At the beginning of his illness, Schreber spent nearly two years in a catatonic state, in which the world, for him, had catastrophically 'disappeared'. Then came the gradual, delusional, reconnection to the world as a 're-libidinisation'.[40]

The Schreber case is also important for

Lacan's theory of psychosis. Among other things, he focuses on the fact that Schreber's rays have a law that they must speak, while much of his delusional content refers to issues of language, such as the existence in God of a 'basic language', as well as the importance of various names. The Schreber case proves, for Lacan, that libido is not to be conceived as just an amorphous and unstructured kind of energy, but that it is articulated in some way through the language structure. Hence any theory of libido has to take account of the nature of the human subject. Lacan himself in his papers on psychosis offers a highly complex picture of how the subject's structure is distorted in psychosis, with various alterations in the relations with reality and in the language structure (Lacan, 1966).[41]

These various issues concerned with the nature of psychosis lead us on to Freud's complex revision of his earlier libido theory with the full introduction of the concept of narcissism in 1914.

Narcissism and Libido/Self and Love

Prior to the narcissism paper, Freud divided the drives into two basic kinds – ego drives and sexual drives. Ego drives were the drives of self-preservation, such as hunger; while the sexual drives referred to sexual impulses. All mental occurrences were to be seen as involving a dynamic interplay between these two sorts of drives. Thus neurotic symptoms were a result of sexual impulses being repressed by the subject's ego, whose function was to protect the mind from excessive mental pain; they were a result of the conflict between the self-preservative function of the ego and the sexual drives pressing to be expressed.

The distinction between the drives of self-preservation and those involving sexuality can be seen already with the infant sucking at the breast. This sucking is first of all associated with the satisfaction of the need for nourishment. But the child's lips also behave like an erotogenic zone, with the flow of warm milk causing pleasurable sensations, the prototype of sexual satisfaction. Freud describes how sexual activity thus attaches itself at the beginning to functions serving the purpose of self-preservation, and does not become independent until later.

No one who has seen a baby sinking back satiated from the breast and falling asleep with flushed cheeks and a blissful smile can escape the reflection that this picture persists as a prototype of the sexual satisfaction in later life.[42] (Freud, 1905)

While feeding requires an object, the breast, to satisfy hunger, sexual feelings are satisfied by a part of the subject's own body, such as the mouth; that is, sexual feelings at this stage are auto-erotic. The need for repeating sexual satisfaction becomes detached from the need to feed, so that sexuality, originally 'leaning on' the self-preservative functions, becomes independent of them at a later stage. Thus sexuality arises from body functioning, yet then becomes detached from its bodily origins.

Whether or not we accept Freud's theory of drives and their origins, the point is that the theory is designed to provide a basic duality for mental functioning. Without this duality it would be hard to explain mental conflict. Ego drives, based on self-preservation, are to be seen as more based on reality – on the need and ability to obtain food and supplies, and to avoid pain. While the sexual drives are more under the dominance of the pleasure principle – they are less susceptible to reality, more intent on seeking gratification. The libido remains under the dominance of the pleasure principle so long because of its ability to escape frustration through auto-erotism; satisfaction can be prolonged, in phantasy, by means of the repetition of auto-erotic activity, originally by sucking, and then later by masturbation.

Freud then describes how a major advance in understanding the nature of the psyche took place with observations from the analysis of psychotic disorders and the introduction of the term 'narcissism', and, with it, the definition of a new and complex duality – between ego-libido and object-libido.

The analysis of psychotic disorders revealed that the ego was not merely an agency of repression and avoidance of pain, but that libido was also attached to it. Thus, as could be seen in the schizophrenic patient described above, who had withdrawn libido from his objects, from other people, and was almost totally preoccupied with himself, it is possible to pathologically transfer onto oneself virtually the whole of the libido which in normal people is directed outwards towards the world and others. That is, the libido can be attached or 'invested' in various ways, either onto the self or onto others. The libido that has been withdrawn from the external world and has been directed towards the ego gives rise to the attitude of narcissism, or 'self-love' in ordinary language. Thus the self-preservative drives are, like the sexual drives, of a libidinal nature; they are sexual drives which, instead of external objects, take the subject's own ego as an object. This libido of the self-preservative drives is now described as 'narcissistic libido'. However, the ego usually does also retain a certain amount of purely self-preservative drives which are unattached to sexual drives; without this, hunger, for example, would always be sexualised. One can see in anorexics how there is a real confusion between food and sexuality. For example, by not eating, in a sense they do not wish to mature sexually; their periods stop, and occasionally in severe cases they may even delay sexual maturation in early adolescence. This is a real, contemporary issue, in that the fashion industry seems obsessed with images of thinness, putting considerable pressure on adolescent girls to keep thin by excessive dieting. One can see here how individual pathology and the social environment are in constant interaction. It is uncertain how much the existence of anorexia is a function of society's expectations about the look of the female body, and how much it would be a problem regardless of advertising pressure.

As for the origin of narcissism, Freud adds that

the megalomania of the narcissistic patient is itself no new creation: it is a magnification of a situation that existed early in life, when the young child was at a stage when they over-estimated the power of their wishes, and felt that they were the centre of the universe; that is, Freud postulates a stage of 'primary' narcissism, when auto-erotism was at its height. Thus the narcissism which has resulted from the with-drawal of libido from objects onto the ego is a secondary one imposed upon a primary nar-cissism.

We can now see that there was an original amount of libido attached to the ego, that the ego is a great 'reservoir' of libido, from which some is later given off to objects, forming object-libido. Freud pictures the relation of ego-libido to object-libido through an analogy taken from zoology:

Think of those simplest of living organisms [the amoebas] *which consist of a little-differentiated globule of protoplasmic substance. They put out protrusions, known as pseudopodia, into which they cause the substance of their body to flow over. They are able, however, to withdraw the protrusions once more and form themselves again into a globule. We compare the putting-out of these protrusions, then, to the emission of libido on to objects while the main mass of libido can remain in the ego; and we suppose that in normal circumstances ego-libido can be transformed unhindered into object-libido and that this can once more be taken back into the ego.*[43]

Thus, instead of the existence of a conflict between ego drives and sexual drives, we now have a conflict between ego-libido and object-libido, with a constant see-saw between the two. With this new duality, Freud can explain both abnormal states – as seen in psychosis, with an extreme withdrawal of libido from objects, and hypochondriasis, when libido becomes attached to the subject's body or a part of the body – and also some normal ones, such as falling asleep, when the subject turns away from the world, withdrawing libido from objects and back into the ego. Being in love consists of an intense flowing-over of ego-libido on to the loved object. Indeed, the megalomania of the psychotic patient is, in Freud's words:

. . . *in every way comparable to the familiar sexual overvaluation of the object in* [normal] *erotic life. In this way for the first time we learnt to understand a trait in a psychotic illness by relating it to normal erotic life.*[44]

While Freud postulates a state of primary narcissism, when the infant's libido is virtually unattached to objects, subsequent thinkers have emphasised that it is impossible to view the infant as unattached to an object; that the infant is always related to some extent. Only in the uterus could one conceive of the possibility of a primary narcissism, and, even there, there may be the possibility of an awareness of the mother – if only through the loud presence of the maternal heart-beat.

Thus, Donald Winnicott emphasises that it is impossible to think of an infant without bringing in its mother; that it is more accurate to picture the mother–infant dyad as primary, rather than the infant themselves unattached to an object.[45] Most analysts since then have also added the notion of a relationship between the subject and the other to any consideration of sexual development – something which is there in Freud and Abraham, but which had been relatively undeveloped by other theorists.

The Human Subject and the Drives/ The Transformational Pathway

In the 'Three Essays', we have seen how, for Freud, the subject can gradually, through development, organise the drives. What is proposed in this final section is a way of understanding more about the subject as a 'libidinal subject', or as organiser of the drives.

Freud describes how the drives in childhood are not unified but consist of a number of different components, or 'partial' drives, each with a special libidinal connection to an erotogenic zone, a part of the body giving rise to a form of sexual excitation. Using evidence from, for example, the perversions where the partial drives fall apart, Freud describes how usually the sexual drive is put together from the various partial drives into what he calls a 'firm organisation'. This happens only at puberty, when the primacy of the genitals is finally beginning to be established, and sexual maturity, the capacity to impregnate and to be impregnated, occurs. The erotogenic zones then fit themselves into this new arrangement, with the genital zone as the leading zone. The new organisation is a result of the combination of the partial drives into a unity by the adolescent subject.

Freud's drive theory thus points towards the way that the subject may become organised, or disorganised if things do not go well, at adolescence. As Laufer and Laufer (1984) have pointed out, the unity of the mature body image at this time has a crucial role in creating the final sexual organisation.[46] What usually takes place is the integration of the old and the new, coming to terms with the loss of the old immature body image and accepting the libidinal investment of the new maturing body image. However, there may occur a breakdown in the process of integrating the mature body image into the subject, with an accompanying fragmentation of the mind and the production of various symptoms, including suicidal feelings, anorexia, and overt psychotic breakdown, as was outlined in the case of Simon above.

While the task of integrating the body image is important in synthesising the partial drives, Freud, in his paper 'Instincts and their Vicissitudes', reveals other ways in which the subject relates to others, and shows how the subject is transformed in various ways by the drive. He seems to describe an elaborate relationship between the subject and the drives, where the subject appears and disappears at various points in the complicated route or circuit of the drive. Although the ultimate aim of each drive is to seek satisfaction, there may be different paths leading to the same aim, and various aims may be combined and interchanged with one another, reflecting once more the fluidity of the libido.

To tie down some of these routes with regard to the sexual drives, Freud examines – in detail – perversions such as sadomasochism. He traces how the sexual drive, experienced as sexual enjoyment, weaves its way through the relations between two subjects, such as the sadist and the masochist. The position each subject takes in relation to the other subject, that of the sadist to the masochist and vice versa, will direct the drive and transform it in various ways. Sexual enjoyment is different if one takes up the sadistic position as opposed to the masochistic one, though there is also overlap.

Such situations reveal the presence of what we could call a 'transformational pathway' between subjects.[47] The subject appears and disappears at various points in a complicated drive circuit; the drive can transform the subject, and the subject can transform the drive. In this sense, we can see

that libido as the 'driving force' behind the drive
can find a place in contemporary psychoanalytic
theory, but as one element of a pathway leading
back and forth from an essentially libidinal
human subject.

The philosopher Herbert Marcuse develops
Freud's theory of libido, with a mixture of his
own brand of Marxism, for an attack on the
way that modern civilisation has become too
repressive.[48] Freud described how civilisation
required that the sexual drives be repressed so
that humans could work effectively. Marcuse
argued that this may have been necessary so long
as basic commodities were scarce, but became
unnecessary once modern technology could
satisfy our needs without repression. Unpleasant
work could now be kept to a minimum, and so
we no longer have to thwart our sexuality. His
revolutionary vision of a new society is one in
which the libido is liberated, no longer having
to conform to the excessive demands of a
repressive civilisation. Instead, we would have a
'libidinous' civilisation, which would dissolve

repressive institutions, allow more time for pleasure and enjoyment, and eliminate alienated labour.

Though Marcuse is not too clear about how such a society could be maintained, his vision of a new relation to sexuality has been influential; it was one of the guiding principles of the sixties' student movements. While such a vision may now seem hopelessly Utopian in our material-istic 'market' culture, perhaps we need to give more room to the notion of libido. Without it, we run the risk of losing our subjectivity in the quest for material gain.

Notes

1. Freud, S., 'Three Essays on the Theory of Sexuality' (1905), *Standard Edition of the Complete Psychological Works of Sigmund Freud*, London: Hogarth Press, 1953–73 (hereafter referred to as *SE*), vol. VII, p. 217.

2. Jacques Lacan (1901–81) was an influential and controversial French psychoanalyst. His main aim was to restore psychoanalysis to life by a radical re-interpretation of Freud's thought, and by putting psychoanalysis in touch with contemporary thought. Though forming his own school of psychoanalysis, he has had considerable influence on analysts in France and elsewhere. See Benvenuto, B. and Kennedy, R., *The Works of Jacques Lacan* (London: Free Association Books, 1986), for an introduction to his thought.

3. Lacan, J., *The Seminar of Jacques Lacan*, Book 2, ed. J.-A. Miller, trans. S. Tomaselli, Cambridge: Cambridge University Press, 1978, pp. 221–2.

4. Freud, S., 'Wild Psychoanalysis' (1910), *SE*, vol. XI, p. 223.

5. Freud, S., 'Instincts and their Vicissitudes' (1915), *SE*, vol. XIV, p. 117. Although the German word *Triebe* is translated in the official title as 'Instincts', a more accurate translation would be 'Drives'.

6. Freud, S., 'Group Psychology and the Analysis of the Ego' (1921), *SE*, vol. XVIII, p. 90.

7. Sophocles, *Women of Trachis*, trans. E. Watling, Harmondsworth: Penguin, 1953, p. 136.

8. Sophocles, *Antigone*, trans. E. Watling, Harmondsworth: Penguin, 1947, p. 148.

9. Laplanche, J. and Pontalis, J.-B., *The Language of Psychoanalysis*, trans. D. Nicholson-Smith, London: Hogarth Press, 1967, p. 277.

10. Kohon, G., *The British School of Psychoanalysis: The Independent Tradition*, London: Free Association Books, 1986, p. 20.

11. Green, A., 'Has Sexuality Anything to Do with Psychoanalysis?', *International Journal of Psychoanalysis*, vol. 76, part 5, 1995, pp. 871–83.

12. Lacan, J., *The Four Fundamental Concepts of Psychoanalysis*, Harmondsworth: Penguin Books, 1973, p. 153.

13. Mollon, P., *The Unconscious*, 'Ideas in Psychoanalysis' series, Cambridge: Icon Books, 2000, pp. 62–4.

14. Kohon, G., op. cit., and Kohon, G., *No lost certainties to be found*, London: Karnac Books, 1999.

15. Freud, S., *The Complete Letters of Sigmund Freud to Wilhelm Fliess*, trans. and ed. J. Masson,

London and Cambridge, MA: Harvard University Press, 1985, p. 80.

16. Ibid., p. 80.

17. Ibid., pp. 80–1.

18. Freud, S. (1905), op. cit., p. 133.

19. Ibid., p. 170.

20. Freud, S., 'Introductory Lectures on Psychoanalysis' (1916–17), *SE*, vol. XVI, p. 348.

21. Freud, S., 'Types of Onset of Neurosis' (1912), *SE*, vol. XII, p. 231.

22. Ibid., p. 232.

23. Ibid., pp. 233–4.

24. Ibid., p. 236.

25. Ibid., p. 236.

26. Freud, S. (1905), op. cit., p. 186.

27. Proust, M., *Time Regained* (1927), trans. A. Meyer, London: Chatto and Windus, 1972, p. 267.

28. Freud, S. (1985), op. cit., p. 207.

29. Freud, S., 'Screen Memories' (1899), *SE*, vol. III, p. 322.

30. Freud, S., 'From the History of an Infantile Neurosis' (1918), *SE*, vol. XVII, p. 45n.

31. Freud, S. (1905), op. cit., p. 234.

32. Lacan, J., *Écrits* (1966), trans. A. Sheridan, London: Tavistock, 1977, p. 52.

33. Ibid., pp. 52–3.

34. See Klein, M., 'Notes on Some Schizoid Mechanisms' (1946), in Klein, M., *Envy and Gratitude and Other Works, 1946–63*, London: Hogarth Press, 1980.

35. Freud. S., 'The Disposition to Obsessional Neurosis' (1913), *SE*, vol. XII, p. 320.

36. Ibid., p. 320.

37. Ibid., pp. 321–2.

38. Abraham, K., 'The First Pregenital Stage of the Libido' (1916), *Selected Papers of Karl Abraham*, trans. D. Bryan and A. Strachey, London: Hogarth Press, 1927, pp. 254–5.

39. Ibid., p. 257.

40. Freud, S., 'Psychoanalytical Notes on an Autobiographical Account of a Case of Paranoia' (1912), *SE*, vol. XII, p. 70.

41. Lacan, J. (1966), op. cit., p. 199ff.

42. Freud, S. (1905), op. cit., p. 182.

43. Freud, S. (1916–17), op. cit., p. 416.

44. Ibid., p. 415.

45. See, for example, Winnicott, D., *The Maturational Processes and the Facilitating Environment*, London: Hogarth Press, 1968.

46. Laufer, M. and Laufer, E., *Adolescence and*

Developmental Breakdown, New Haven and London: Yale University Press, 1984.

47. See Kennedy, R., *The Elusive Human Subject*, London: Free Association Books, 1998, pp. 84–90.

48. Marcuse, H., *Eros and Civilization*, London: Allen Lane, 1955, p. 161ff.